ROSE AND THORNS
PETAL THAT BLED POETRY

KANZA KHAN

XpressPublishing
An imprint of Notion Press

No.8, 3rd Cross Street, CIT Colony,
Mylapore, Chennai, Tamil Nadu-600004

Copyright © Kanza Khan
All Rights Reserved.

ISBN 978-1-63669-466-5

This book has been published with all efforts taken to make the material error-free after the consent of the author. However, the author and the publisher do not assume and hereby disclaim any liability to any party for any loss, damage, or disruption caused by errors or omissions, whether such errors or omissions result from negligence, accident, or any other cause.

While every effort has been made to avoid any mistake or omission, this publication is being sold on the condition and understanding that neither the author nor the publishers or printers would be liable in any manner to any person by reason of any mistake or omission in this publication or for any action taken or omitted to be taken or advice rendered or accepted on the basis of this work. For any defect in printing or binding the publishers will be liable only to replace the defective copy by another copy of this work then available.

'To caffeine and sugar, my companions through many long nights of writing.'

Contents

Preface   *vii*

1. I Write About You. Why?   1
2. Until I Met You   3
3. Exploring You   5
4. Just Like That   6
5. I Forgot How To Cry   8
6. Falling For You   9
7. Rare   10
8. Your Eyes   11
9. Twilight   12
10. Destined To Be   14
11. I Choose You   16
12. Came Along   19
13. Confession   20
14. Will You?   22
15. I Was There   23
16. Turning Point   25
17. Couldn't Be   27
18. Chapter 18   28
19. Why?   30
20. Chapter 20   31
21. Jump   33
22. Weak But Got Words To Speak   34
23. Last Call   35

Contents

24. Rise	36
25. Let You Go	37
26. Sleepless	38
27. Negative	40
28. Strength	41
29. Remember To Miss Me	42
30. Goodbye	44

Preface

You're not just holding a book in your hands but a canvas of my emotions where I spilled the ink of poetry expecting it to reach out to thine heart from mine..

A mix of heaven and hell right here on the ground beneath us is how I'd describe what this book is all about. The poems it consists reached my life at different phases.

Read and you won't feel alone in this battle of decisions and consequences, success and failure, love, loss, hatred, grief.. Its all here, We're together.

You aren't alone. I'm with you.

1. I write about you. Why?

You paint the sky of my petrified life in bright mornings with the vibrant colours of your endless love and the thunderous clouds and rains of fear and sorrow vanish away just when the rainbow of our love blooms out from the rivers of trust and loyalty to the flowers of passion and comfort.

With you i got hidden emotions into existence which were always assumed won't be there.

You got me hypnotic and fascinating to yourself and everything about you. From the strand of your hair when you're out from hot showers to the droplets of water on your breathtaking and radiant skin chest. From your bewitching eyes that hold mysteries in them which i would spend this lifetime in finding about to the mesmerizing cuts on either sides of your waist. From the veins on your arms to the dimples on your cheeks . I am obsessed with all of it.

You bring exquisite evenings to enchanted passionate nights of love between both of our bodies when they become one.

You connect with me not just with intertwined hands and bodies but souls; Tangled enough to not get separated no matter what evils come between.

You hold me at my worst and redefine it with the best possible.

I am more of me when I'm with you. So I'll write about you

till there's no words left. I'll write about you when we define perfect. I'll write about you and make them believe we were and we are. We will always be long after we're both gone. The taste of these words will linger forever on every soul who claims to be in love. I will write about you and write about what love did to us. How beautiful can this word be when felt with purity. The story us will have every page of me and you falling in deep knowing there's no way out. On the last sentence I'll shout it out, I love you, forever and always, I did and always will.

2. Until I met you

Of many words, I now have none
I can't figure out how it begun
Of a billion people out there
My heart raced for one
If only words were enough
To tell, what a gem you are
The sole being, known to each of my scar
I'd hold you forever but you're so far
Just when I gave up on love
Thought it wasn't for me
Then along you came to set me free
With a love of 9 long years
Vanishing all my fears
Holding my face,
Wiping my tears.
All the broken parts of me
The one's, this world couldn't see
You pulled up the disguise
I wore of a happy life
You held me in your arms
And healed them with your care and charm.
I knew not of true love
Until I met you

Since then in a better person for us I've grew
In the spaces between each breath
With every moment I live
My heart, my soul, my mind
You look through them, your name you'll find.
We knew not of destiny and fate
When we've been through struggle and hate
Now I know it was for something great
When I saw you my love, my soulmate

3. Exploring you

I've seen under your hard shell and saw the vulnerable layers. I've heard the trembling of tender words when you felt so much.
I've known your laughter, I've kissed away your tears. I've experienced trauma with you, I've felt your pain. I touched you like a rose flower when I knew of thorns too and got magnetized to it. I seek you for the warmth of love that beats in your chest when you keep it hidden on cold days. I saw you breaking, I watched you rise again. I witnessed the best and worst with you of us. I've loved you as a mix of heaven and hell with heart of an angel and it can't get any better. You can't be any more perfect than you really are. I've beheld the beauty of a soul like yours to which no words could describe the perfection of it. I've known you more than you, I'm still exploring you..

4. Just like that

I want to be the lyrics of your favourite song that doesn't get out of your head. I want to be the fragrance on your body that makes you so perfect. I want to be the sunshine that falls on your face and gleams up your skin. I want to be the reason that pushes you to keep trying even at your worst. I want to be the silence in your words and understand it. I want to be the one you turn to when life gets hard. I want to be the most beautiful reminiscence of your life.
I want to be the one holding you when nightmares scare you. I want to be someone who makes you believe in heaven on earth.
I want to be worth taking risks with. I want to be who you trust blindly. I want to be the one who soothes your thirst for love,care,honesty loyalty. I want to be the magic you believe in when i move the wand of my love for you and makes things alright. I want to stop time when we are together and want you to feel the same. I want to be the thorn on the rose you are and keep others away who try to pluck off your train of perfection. I want you to grow with me and achieve your goals. I want to cherish you with titbits of my efforts and make big differences and gaze your adorable face when you smile that lights up my world. I want to be the breathes you grasp for when it feels like you're drowning. I want my hand

to hold yours and take you out safe and sound. I want to be knowing about your insecurities and fears.

I want to be with you in all your vulnerability and craziness. I want to be the love, the love that your heart beats for. I want to be yours

I want to be with the real you, all masks off.

5. I forgot how to cry

When I see you looking at me
Swear to god it sets my heart free
Everytime you touch my hair
Caressing them with utmost care
Boy you got me flying high
Heaven on earth I forgot how to cry
Waking up beside you day and night
We live above wrong and right
There's sole joy no room for pain
You protect me from every storm and rain
Boy you got me flying high
Heaven on earth I forgot how to cry

6. Falling for you

You are every bit of me, not you but me, that matters the most. Matters more than the need of having warm mornings when nights are too cold and horrible and scary; if you're beside, you'll make it beautifully bearable. You matter more than making wish upon a shooting star because what's left to ask for when I have you already.
All of my wishes that I wanted to fulfill in this lifetime now revolve around you. I want to live each of them slowly.. patiently with every stage of our lives together.
You matter more than any soul I've ever known in life. My priorities, my decisions, my deeds, my thoughts, my love, my body, my soul, every atom that's mine belongs to you.
I want to love you on dark days and be your hope of light. I want to hold you when you're the most vulnerable version of yourself.
I want to wrap my arms around you, tell you it'll be alright not with words but kisses on your forehead and cheeks.
Anything in this world isn't valuable more than the smile of your juicy lips when they paint a ray of sunshine on the most darkest parts of me and melt the cold walls I've built. Any pain or grief can be endured as long as I have you and your captivating contagious smile and those dimples! I just fell for it again!

7. Rare

You love with freckles of bad experiences, broken promises, betrayed feelings, unsaid words, hidden dark secrets, scared emotions, terrifying past, absurd childhood, faded memories, losing loved one's,missed chances, regrets of not trying, fear of rejection

You love with stolen moments of love, slow kisses, daydreaming, passionate nights, caring days,warm hugs, little things that give bright smiles, holding hands with hesitation hoping it'll be held tighter, breathes on lover's neck, desires to trace their soul before skin, hopes to know him/her in ways no one else could, exploring the depths of who they are in real when nobody's around, wish upon a shooting star to make love to the heart before bodies. You love unlike no other. You love rare. You are, rare.

8. Your eyes

Your eyes,looks like rays of sunshine,looks like honey dripped right in there, looks like the ocean's changed colour to brown and golden when the sun sets, looks like the bronze jewels who's worth can't be decided as it exceeds what one can give to keep them, looks like autumn and old trees, your eyes hold stories and secrets, have watched the best and worse of love and hatred, witnessed twist and turns of life, your eyes saw rise and fall, your eyes spoke when words were too small. Your eyes made love before your hands reached, your eyes could see the invisible parts of me, your eyes, where I saw my today and all of my tomorrows. You eyes took away all of my sorrows

9. Twilight

My lips stroll on your sultry soft skin
I close my eyes and see the smooth cuts of your waist
Fingers caressing you, back and forth as if polishing the porcelain surface of a statue who's made to be mine
Yearning for my attention, touch
Strings of a harp waiting to make music,
My canvas , your desirable body
I paint, love and passion on each inch of you
I meet your lips and your hands intertwine in mine to answer my craving
I seductively brush your neck with feathers, make you come closer
Intensifying the raging desire of bodies to become one
Remnants saliva painted with my tongue evaporates into more of a magnetism and you, you can't let it go, it works like magic
I pour you with my weight of heated passion and dreams to be lived
Our tongues dance to the rhythm of our beating hearts and my legs envelop you
I watch you lose yourself in the heat of the moment, now two bodies are one
I continue to breath on your neck and watch you pant heavy

I rise up and come down, your weight on me I love
And with a burning wave of passion,
Enfolded bodies met heaven

10. Destined to be

I've spent days dreaming
And nights not sleeping
What would it take
to make you mine?
The darkest hours
Led me nowhere
And this was never fine
Then one day
Out of the blue
In my sight
I saw you
I walked steps forward
You ran to me
This was the answer,
Now I can see
You held me in your arms
The world stopped for a while
Intrigued by your charm
Lost my heart, a little too fragile
Knowing you'd keep it best
Somewhere hidden, a treasure chest
You gave your heart and love and care
Not a moment without them we'd spare

For you, for me
A perfect us
It was destined to be.

11. I choose you

Where will I wander one lonely night when the world is asleep and no soul bothers to see mine roaming on the streets shivering in cold winds blowing away my hopes of finding warmth after walking miles trying to get drunk on my emotions till I feel no more but then I stop by,Ii stop by a building where lives a guy I've known for years. He isn't among the one's you get a glance of and forget the next moment. His face stays stuck in your heart and the personality doesn't leave your mind. The one you'd meet after years and still be able to say "you didn't change at all", "your lips are just like before". You meet him and realize you've reached the warmth you've been craving for.

You see him and it's hard to believe that someone like him exists in the chaotic cruel word that holds on nothing but heartbreaks, betrayal,depression,anxiety, feelings that are left unsaid or if shared then left being ignored, not valued. But this person comes to you with bright hopes that you deep down believe aren't fake. He opens his arms welcoming you in his aura occupied with endless love, unconditional care,sensuous passion, real promises of loyalty and trust and there you are stuck standing still,not being able to move because someone like him hasn't crossed your path in years since he left once, things that went away with him, came back being the best you could've asked for. You need to settle in, accept that this is happening to you, life is joining back the pieces of you both that were broken. His soul mends yours. You know it, you're feeling it but you're lost in the moment when you have flashbacks of the time when he was yours and things were perfect because all this time, this human is still yours. How on earth can a person like me deserve abundance of luck and happiness all at once?! Was that a dream I'm writing about? Clearly not. I couldn't have imagined this perfection in a person giving me all the happiness, much more than think i deserve from the day he accepted my chaos as his, felt my emotions in his heart. Got hurt when I'm in pain. Understood silence when i couldn't utter words. Wrapped my troubled soul in his arms to make me believe he's there and nothing can shake both of your happiness when we're together. It wasn't a dream else i wouldn't have been awake. I lived a reality and continue to live it everyday. The warmth of his arms, the softness of his lips, the future in his hands. I have it all. The lonely night is over. The world is awake yet makes no change. The cold winds don't bother anymore. The warmth is found. The love is kept safe. Now I'm not the only soul roaming on streets, obviously not the one trying to kill emotions. He stands with me, walks not too slow neither pacing up leaving me behind. Just beside. We are the one's to navigate through life's ups and downs together always. Till? There's no such word that decides when we end. Name it timeless, because we are.

In a hundred lifetimes in any version of reality I'd find you and I'd choose you.

12. Came along

The flowers never bloomed so bright
Moon has shone with all its might
On each broken star I wish
Maybe being too selfish
To make you stay
As long as there's night and day
To hold you hand
And to never lose the grip
To be held by you
the moment I trip
To hug you tight enough
That you forget
What it feels like to have any regret
To kiss out the grief inside you
To end the days so blue
To make your nights no less than what you dream
To show the world together we're the best team
To make you believe, its always been you
To end up the distances if there's still a few

13. Confession

It is time
I shouldn't hide it anymore
Gather up courage
And stand at your door
It's been a while with you
I know I get high with you
But this time
I'm all sane
Since the day we met
I've let go of my pain
It's no joke
The words are true
Maybe a little more than yours
My feelings have grew
This ain't easy to confess
But I had no other way
So hear me when I say
Since I met your eyes
Saw you everywhere in disguise
You're the blood to my heart
There's nothing keeping us apart
Don't wanna lose you ever
You're all for me

Call me possessive, call me clever
Things won't be like before
Cause now you know, You're the one I adore
My other half I want you to be
A perfect future of us,
Is all I see

14. Will you?

Will you place your hand on my burning forehead when I'm sick?
Will you hold me when I fall apart?
Will you defend me in public without hesitations or fear of being judged?
Will you trust me when the world turns its back on me?
Will you stand by me even if I become nothing but a troublemaker to your life?
Will you kiss me when I'm asleep?
Will you catch me when I fall?
Will you touch my heart and feel the beat when it gets rapid?
Will you console me when I go breathless while crying?
Will you try to find only my hands to hold when you're weak?
Will you be an open book to me?
Will you answer all of my curiosities and concerns?
Will you stay by my side even if you feel I'm wrong?
Will you love me when I give you reasons not to?
Will you walk through all ups and downs and never give up?
Will you love me, always?
Will you stay, always?
Will you believe in us, always?
Will you, will you always?

15. I was there

Somewhere in the corners of the room
when you stare
your eyes gleam with care
you grab her waist
pull her close
gaze her lips and
made a kiss
Intoxicated with your charm
she finds there's no harm
rests on your arm
Serene you both were
until you saw
I was there
On the edge of bursting into tears
With a million questions ; "why dear?"
you take a step towards me
I took a step back
'Cause empathy is what you lack
Devastated and lost
your limits are crossed
Using people for your needs
there's no good just greed
Drowning in sorrow

You'll find no tomorrow

16. Turning point

What's up with you?
Why'd you never call?
Why is it only you
My heart knows at all
Those midnight conversations,
To handling complications,
To others invasion,
To our separation.
We could've lasted longer
If you had been a little more stronger
It's not about blaming
But what we did for saving?
A bond never seen ever
When did we become so clever?
No, its not just you
But its me too
When those roads remind our walks
Our laughs and never ending talks
Its hurts to see who we were
And what we've become
Just two strangers
Whose paths were same
Now they live in a different fame

Forgetful of each others name.

17. Couldn't be

Seeing him was magic but his favourite act was to disappear.And let these memories keep me awake at night the way he did doing nothing but pouring our hearts out and craving to see each other,grabbing the whole damn world in our arms and then holding hands he'd say "Babe..we made it.. despite the problems we faced and times we thought of giving up but didn't because WE are meant to be"

Unlike now when I got no idea what he's upto and little does he know bad it gets when he's not by my side. It feels like the sky rains just to make hiding tears a lot easier for me

The dark night shows no beauty of the moon anymore but its loneliness even among those infinite stars.. So here I lay alone teaming up with the moon sharing my dark secrets which were once shared with you

Though we're apart but I hope one day when there's no more chaos, no taunts, no arguments, no secrets, and no one between the two of us

We'll meet.. and make our dreams come true

In a world full of people struggling to love

We would show how to fall in love immensely and be loved back even more.

Nothing values more than you being with a mess like me.

Chapter 18

Another gloomy night
Sitting by the window
Ogling the blue sky
Riveted by the moon
Standing still amongst millions of stars
Reliant on him to appear and shine
Those millions out there
and there's this one thing
not so perfect,
not luminating, yet
stays there with flaws
Never ashamed of those marks
Well known to his worth
The sky is just zilch without him
He's far from perfect
But gazing him
is worth it.
Remember crying to him
Ranting about all of your life issues
Isn't he the best listener; keeper
A log of yours and the world's dark secrets
To me this is his life purpose
He wasn't given light of his own

Instead he is the silent guide
who does nothing but lightens up your ways
when you're tired of yelling and at last commit to lift your spirits again
Only because he heard you cry , your emotions , difficulties, sorrow
You didn't need to saved by him or anyone but just needed to someone to be there and listen
He's the moon. Did that

19. Why?

I lay still at nights when loving you seems to be a trauma I can't get enough of
To this day I couldn't explain it to myself
Was it just me ?
Was it just you ?
Were you nothing but a mirage of dreams
I remember gazing those bewitching brown eyes of yours
As if there was nothing left to desire for
I could drown in them deep and deep knowing there's no rescue out

Chapter 20

I'm lost in your memories
Come find me
Show me the right path
Save me from this world
Take me somewhere far
Beyond right and wrong
Above love and hate
A place with no chaos
No emotions no pain
No sobbing no waiting
And if you could
Then stay there until
I fall asleep in your arms
and please don't leave me sleeping
I am scared
Terrified of nightmares
Then what if I wake up
Will you stay for more
or leave from the exit door?
Oh love I'm scared
Terrified of nightmares
Sing me to an eternal sleep
For I know you won't stay

But do come see me someday
In a river of dreams is where I lay
Hold my hand and pull me close
Say you chose me and didn't care of what the world will say
Oh love I'm scared
Terrified of nightmares

21. Jump

I count to 1 2 3
Jump in a deep wide sea
Those creatures staring at me
It's not my place to be
I move along with them
As my presence they condemn
I'm here for a short while
Won't swim another mile

22. Weak but got words to speak

Is it better if I say that
Or should I keep shut
"Look at my smile
Not that bruise and cut"
Weak , fragile whatever you name
You might be strong
But I'm not the same
Yes. I get weak
Still I've got words to speak
Yet you can't hear
Even with that ear
That catches only gossips and fears
Then god forbid that filthy mouth of yours
Rumours and fake judgments
Reasons for my tears.

23. Last call

Been holdin' onto you
For a long while
Can't forget your last smile
When you told me to wait
I stood close to the gate
Holding onto you , on to you, I
Keep staring on the way
Hoping you'd return
Been holding onto what you say,
"I'll be back to you
I got some works to do
I know the path is long
I swear not to do you any wrong"
But boy now let me speak
My patience's on it's peak
Cause I've been holding on
Ever since you've been gone
I couldn't wait no more
This is the last call of mine
I hope wherever you are
You'd be fine.

24. Rise

Sinking, I'm sinking
Deeper and deeper
The mistakes I did being a disbeliever
Don't wanna look back
Don't want to stop
My past is drowning me
A little drop by drop
Tryna be better than I was before
Give life to the old me;
The one you adore
But I need some time
Give me some space
I need to wash this guilt off my face
It troubles me to the core
Keeps me awake till 4
I'm looking for ways to end being a disgrace But I'll make this right
Just keep calm, stay quiet and polite

25. Let you go

Gonna keep it to myself
Won't let you know
All the truths that I hide
And feelings I don't show
I don't hate you
No no no
I'm just keeping it real low
Cause I can love you and still let you go

26. Sleepless

I don't want these long nights
Laying and blaming
Thinking and dreaming
Craving and Screaming
Loving and breathing
All of you for her
None of you for me
Take a moment
And look back
I'm still
Standing and waiting
Still loving and breathing
Pacing back and forth
You didn't return
I'm tired
So I turn around
Loneliness surround
Running and crying
Losing breathes but trying
Under the sheer dark sky
Gazing the stars up in high
Night at its peak
I am

Not so loving just breathing
In the arms of winds I lay
To fall asleep I pray

27. Negative

Light a fire in the dark
Show me who you are
Unfold sleeves hiding that scar
And all your sinful desire
Things you do in despair
When you choke to almost death
There's no one to care
Echoing voices in head
Screaming yet no sound
Losing hopes as tears shed
Ought to suffer for this is where you're bound

28. Strength

I wore that strength of inside of me
Battling wars of emotions and reality
Hiding of what killed me a million times
Keeping my demons under control
Holding onto what I've survived
the spirit that kept me alive
This girl is a mystery -
full of question marks
And with eyes lighting sparks
A pro in turning tables
You go in for answers
She changes the question
She's the kind of Paradise
you crave to live in
Yet a result of hell she's been through
Coming out as a warrior
She's capable of bleeding you to death
But for her revenge is a different story
Fears no power, lives for none
Just one glance of her
And you're done.

29. Remember to miss me

When liquid courage spills out our truth
When you grab her close, there's my face you see
Oh Pretty boy, remember to miss me
She pulls your hand, and dives in the pool
The water drops run down your bodies
You can feel her curves more seductive
The intense fire gets obsessive
You're getting closer baby
Do you remember to miss me?
When I caught your attention with wet hair strands down my waist, full clothes on
When you ran after trying to hold me
Do you remember?
Remember to miss me?
The mansion is huge, the life's luxurious
Your desires turned to reality
Is there still a place for the little dreams you see
Keeping it hidden when she's laying besides
Your mind, heart, thoughts, where all our memories reside
You fake your rigid and cold
I visit your dreams, you melt in my arms
Don't worry, there's nobody I've told
But spill the hatred to my face

Look in my eyes and say it out loud
Is she, she the one for you?
Let me hold your hand and ask
Is that really true?
Whatever the answer may be
Remember.. remember to miss me

30. Goodbye

Promising 'forevers' is not what I need
promise me your presence
sitting beside me when I lay
eyes closed, cold blooded, dried lips
whispering out the love this heart has ever felt
promise to remember me
when I'm far far away
twinkling with billions of other stars
watching you from above
being proud to have lived a life with you
and cursing myself for being able to have you in my arms a little while more
your love for me is what I adore
promise me just promise me
Promise me that you'll keep all of your promises
I promise to be the spark in your eyes,
the smile to your face, the blush on your cheeks
I promise to embrace your name till my lungs give out
Standing on the seventh sky my heart will shout
I'm done with my breathes
never done with you
you lifted me to the skies
and cherished the moments we lived

Now I gotta leave
But you stay safe and sound
And believe I'm always around
Here I am waving goodbye
To the love that will never
die..

A million thank you's to each and every soul who made an effort to go through the glimpses of my life by reading the words I sewed with utmost passion and hardwork.

THANK YOU SO MUCH!

www.ingramcontent.com/pod-product-compliance
Lightning Source LLC
LaVergne TN
LVHW041547060526
838200LV00037B/1185